Before it all began. The former trackbed of the standard gauge line from Bangor to Afonwen on the south side of Caernarfon tunnel in 1994. The new WHR station now occupies this site.

The station site at Dinas in 1994, when still occupied by the local authority's civil engineering department. Several of the temporary buildings in the photo were removed before tracklaying began in early 1997.

The old station building at Waunfawr in 1994. After the closure of the WHR in 1936 the building fell more and more into disrepair, and was eventually demolished to make way for the new station platform. It was replaced by a splendid new replacement in the original style in 2019.

The original North Wales Narrow Gauge Railway station building at Snowdon Ranger taken in 1994. It was sold privately as a holiday cottage during the closure period and does not form part of the modern Welsh Highland Railway.

The road and rail bridge at Pont Croesor after completion of road improvements. The pillars to the left were from the original railway and were re-used during Phase 4 of the WHR reconstruction.

The site of Portmadoc (New) 1923 station taken in 1994. The concrete pillars of the old water tower are still there, and the crumpled heap of corrugated iron to its right is all that remains of the old station building, destroyed by fire in 1990.

The WHR Funkey 335hp diesel at Minffordd Yard in 1995, as received from a cement factory in South Africa. After receiving attention it was painted in maroon livery and given the name CASTELL CAERNARFON. It has given sterling service ever since.

The WHR acquired NGG16 Beyer-Garratt locomotives from South Africa to haul heavy trains over the steep gradients of the WHR. This one, No.140 was acquired through generous German and Swiss enthusiasts, and was on display at the 1997 FR Gala in Blaenau Ffestiniog.

This Garratt, No.138, was demonstrated at Glan y Pwll depot on the Ffestiniog Railway at the May 1997 Gala Weekend.

By April 1997 redundant buildings had been demolished at Dinas, new platforms constructed on the former standard gauge alignment, and ballast laid in preparation for the beginning of track laying.

April 1997 again, this time looking towards Caernarfon at Dinas. Several South African Railways B wagons can be seen lined up on the bank – they came in very handy as track component containers en route to the UK.

FROM VAN DONNYBROOK
TO NA DINAS JUNCTION
CONTENTS HHOUD COACH SCREWS
TRUCK/ ROK NO. 1834
DATUM ATE 7-8-96
TES TAS from ACR

Two more B wagons at Dinas, outside what is now known as the Clip Shed. Inset is a wagon label from Donnybrook in Natal, rescued by an EAG member from a puddle.

At Dinas in April 1997 could be seen this pile of steel sleepered track panels from Donnybrook in Natal, ready and waiting for tracklaying to commence. In the background is a collection of nine DZ flat wagons which were to prove very useful later on.

On October 4th 1997 the Funkey diesel CASTELL CAERNARFON was busy marshalling stock at Dinas in preparation for the first train to depart for Caernarfon.

The Welsh Highland Railway Society AGM was under way at Y Mount pub on 4th October 1997 when news filtered through that the first steam hauled train from Dinas to Caernarfon was about to depart. Unfortunately, it had to run as empty stock as the Light Railway Order was not yet in force, but there was nonetheless a rapid exit from the meeting to see Garratt 138 leaving!

No.138 approaching St Helens Road overbridge in Caernarfon on the return leg of the first steam hauled empty stock train, bound for Caernarfon (4.10.1997).

A prototype Parry People Mover railcar, powered by propane gas and a large flywheel, was tested on the Ffestiniog Railway in 1997. It is seen here at Boston Lodge.

Early Garratt-hauled services on the former standard gauge portion of the WHR, with its generous clearances, allowed the use of the swing-out cab seats that were a daily feature of the locos' service in South Africa. The seats were removed before services were extended.

A second Parry People Mover railcar, No.11, was demonstrated on the Welsh Highland Railway in 1998. It saw some use on late season services but suffered a breakdown, following which it was removed from the railway, never to return. Dinas, September 1998.

Left: The next phase of reconstruction was the original WHR trackbed between Dinas and Waunfawr. This is the A4085 overbridge at Waunfawr with the station area beyond, September 1999.

Right: Waunfawr station area in September 1999 with the remains of the station building which were taken down shortly afterwards. Although a temporary structure was erected, a brand new replacement in stone had to wait until 2019.

This is the reinstated cutting at Dinas looking back towards the station. The cutting had to be re-excavated and some 80,000 tons of spoil were removed. The brick arch does not match the one on the other side of the bridge. After the railway closed the A487 road across the bridge was widened and some far sighted engineer widened the bridge to the existing dimensions instead of filling it in.

By 25th June 2000 track had been laid beyond Tryfan Junction. Seen here in a view looking back towards Caernarfon, horse riders are crossing the line on the site of the level crossing. The former branch to Bryngwyn curved in from the left.

Seen here at Cae Wernlas Ddu propelling a wagon carrying volunteer tracklayers, WHR stalwart UPNOR CASTLE hoves into sight, driven by Dave Kent. 25.6.2000.

Cae Wernlas Ddu Siding, with recently acquired South African ballast wagons on the WHR main line. The temporary loco shed contains the short-lived Gullick & Dobson track tamping machine. 25.6.2000

Waunfawr station on 25th June 2000. The bridge had to be excavated, deepened and underpinned to produce the "Garratt Dip" necessary to allow these large locomotives to pass under the original structures.

A conducted tour of WHR supporters at Waunfawr on 25.6.2000, showing the extent of tracklaying at that time.

The very first Garratt, No. K1, was repatriated from Tasmania by its makers in 1947 and came to the Ffestiniog in 1966. It had to wait until the WHR reconstruction began for its restoration to working order to start. It required a new boiler and here it is being steam tested at Boston Lodge Works on 15th September 2002.

On 6th April 2008 a special train was organised for supporters of the project to restore Garratt K1. The day was one of sunny intervals and quite pleasant, when suddenly the sky blackened and snow began to fall as she left Caernarfon.

The first and last Garratts to be built by Beyer Peacock in Manchester. K1 from Tasmania on the left and 143 from South Africa behind it. Dinas 6th April 2008.

Owner Mike Hart is at the controls of World War 1 Simplex (435/1917), as it hauls a water bowser at Pitt's Head during the Superpower gala weekend of September 2009.

On the 24th March 2007 a supporters' special train was run as far as Cutting Mawr, above Beddgelert, the furthest extent of the track at that time. Passengers in the main train transferred to lighter weight rolling stock at Rhyd Ddu, as the track beyond had not been consolidated. Here the unusual train headed by Funkey CASTELL CAERNARFON, with Garratt No. 138 in the middle, rounds the curve at Ffridd Isaf near Rhyd Ddu. The train was divided beyond Rhyd Ddu and the front portion taken on by diesels UPNOR CASTLE and CONWAY CASTLE.

The two Planet diesels arrive at Cutting Mawr with the special train on 24th March 2007. Participants were not permitted to alight for safety reasons.

The track between Pont Cae'r Gors and Beddgelert had been ballasted and tamped, so Garratt No.138 could be used for the first time on this stretch for the return leg of the special. The two Planet diesels propelled the train back up the 1 in 40 from Cutting Mawr to Pont Cae'r Gors, where the Garratt took over, and is seen here approaching the summit of the line. 24.3.2007.

On 5th April 2008 another milestone was marked by the running of a special First Train through the Aberglaslyn Pass. The train started at Caernarfon and ran through to Hafod y Llyn where the engines were able to run round the carriages.

On board the first passenger train to pass through the newly constructed station at Beddgelert, on 5th April 2008. The eagle eyed will spot one of the small Hudson wagons rebuilt by the East Anglian Group at the far end of the siding.

The train was headed by Garratt No.143 double heading the Funkey diesel CASTELL CAERNARFON. The diesel was used to draw the train forward at Hafod Llyn, as the loop was incomplete. Boston Lodge Works Manager Tony Williams enjoys the experience!

No.143 and CASTELL CAERNARFON round the curve onto Brynyfelin bridge as they return the special first train through the Pass back to Caernarfon, 5.4.2008.

On 16th May 2009 a special train ran as far as Cae Pawb crossing on the outskirts of Porthmadog, the point where the WHR crosses the Cambrian main line. The train was hauled by newly restored Garratt No.87, seen here on the return journey in its early "works grey" livery.

On the outward journey the carriage footboards were maybe a little too close for comfort to the heap of ballast at Hafod y Llyn. 16.5.2009.

The Welsh Highland Heritage Railway parallels the Ffestiniog's Welsh Highland Railway between Pen y Mount and Cae Pawb. The WHHR entered into the spirit of the occasion with some parallel running using their attractive Bagnall 0-4-2T GELERT. 16th May 2009.

No.87 stops a few yards short of the crossing with the Cambrian line, the gate in the distance marks the actual spot. 16th May 2009.

On the 30th October 2010 the first through train ran from Caernarfon to Porthmadog – a truly momentous event marking the completion of the whole line. The late John Keylock brought an original roof board from the "old WHR", and for the occasion displayed it in the window of the observation car on the outward trip.

The first train to Porthmadog from Caernarfon approaching Plas y Nant on the outward trip. 30.10.2010.

The train was forced to halt briefly on the approach to Pont Croesor as a protestor blocked the line with his lorry, but it was quickly removed. 30.10.2010.

A large crowd assembled to watch the train cross the Britannia Bridge in Porthmadog, as it approached Harbour Station. 30.10.2010.

Initially, Welsh Highland trains had to draw onto the Cob before being hauled back into the platform by a pilot engine. Lynton and Barnstaple replica 2-6-2T LYD performed the honours on this occasion, and is buffering up to the observation car. 30.10.2010.

The train engine was Garratt No.138, painted in a smart red livery. Here she is in the siding at Porthmadog Harbour awaiting fuelling and watering in preparation for the return trip. 30.10.2010.

On arrival at Caernarfon, the headboard from the special train was auctioned by Mike Hart, seen holding it aloft. The late and much-missed Eileen Clayton is to his right. 30.10.2010.

Left: A feature of the revived Welsh Highland Railway is the annual fund-raising train, *The Snowdonian*. The train features interesting motive power and runs over the entire route of the Ffestiniog and Welsh Highland Railways. The event on 2nd April 2011 was an all-Fairlie affair. The Ffestiniog portion was headed by TALIESIN and EARL OF MERIONETH, and this is the headboard adorning the former at Porthmadog Harbour.

Above: The Welsh Highland section of the journey featured MERDDIN EMRYS and DAVID LLOYD GEORGE. The pair perform a photographic run-past at Ffridd Isaf, near Rhyd Ddu. 2.4.2011.

An interesting comparison of Fairlie smokeboxes at Beddgelert on *The Snowdonian*. 2.4.2011.

Area groups of the Ffestiniog and Welsh Highland have enjoyed a long history of wagon rebuilding. The WHR East Anglian Group seized a golden opportunity to acquire and rebuild some small Hudson flat wagons from the former 2' gauge line at the Imperial War Museum at Duxford. In better condition than they looked, the wagons were later restored at a site near Cambridge. The airfield fire engine had an interesting 2-4-0 wheel arrangement. Summer 2003.

Four 2'6" gauge wagons from the Royal Navy depot at Beith in Scotland were purchased, and three rebuilt in various forms for the modern Ff&WHR. Nos. 5002 and 5003 were re-gauged, had their frames widened and were fitted with vacuum brakes in our alfresco workshop. The volunteers are Roger Hornsby and the late Tom Skinner. 29.08.2010.

Tom Skinner at work with an angle grinder on one of the MoD wagons. They are used all over the railway system, mainly with the railway's Signals and Telegraph department. One has been to the WHHR at Gelert's Farm, and one has even been spotted in an FR gravity train. 19.09.2009.

Three of the small Hudson wagons from Duxford being rebuilt with raised frames and new central buffers. They saw extensive use on WHR Phase 4 construction trains and one had the 'honour' of being the first rail vehicle to cross the Britannia Bridge in Porthmadog! Mill Green, 19.09.2004.

The Hudson wagons were numbered EAG 1-4 by the Group. In this photo EAG 1 and 4 are seen with newly retimbered decking. Mill Green, Cambs. 28.11.2004.

EAG Hudson wagon no.1 in the siding at the South end of Rhyd Ddu. 7.9.2006.

Dignity and impudence at Rhyd Ddu. The South African ballast wagons tower above poor little EAG1, which seems overloaded with building materials. The yellow vehicle on the left is the ballast plough DAFFODIL. 24.3.2007.

Above: The first MoD wagon to be rebuilt was No.5001, specifically intended as a 'tender' for the KMX Tamper, to keep tools and lubricants away from its sophisticated machinery and electronics. This example does not have vacuum brakes. Rhyd Ddu, 24.3.2007.

Right: The East Anglian Group also made a large number of station running-in boards for the new railway. Unfortunately, the design demanded too much maintenance in a wet climate, and did not stand the test of time. Volunteer Micky Smith poses with the sign for Nantmor Halt. Mill Green, 14.02.2009.

An early Group project was the repainting of the original North Wales Narrow Gauge Railway station building at Dinas, as seen here in 1999.